THE NATURE OF COLOR
IN INTERIOR DESIGN

Gloria Jaroff, AIA

*To Lesley
never
too late
Gloria*

U.S.Copyright © April 2, 2015

Library of Congress Catalog Card No: TXu 1-958-476

Printed U.S. Second Edition, 2016

ISBN 9781515377009

BOOK DESIGNER - Karen Wong

INTERIOR DESIGN - Gloria Jaroff, AIA

SKETCHUP MODELERS - Gloria Jaroff, AIA

Pinky Rose Job

Pedro Calixto

LIGHT RENDERING - Richard Buday, FAIA

EDITING - Richard Buday, FAIA

Dr. Barbara Marantz

LIGHTING CONSULTANT - Kenneth Vick, Lightopia, Manhattan Beach, CA

SUPODIUM CONSULTANTS - David Wayne

Nicolas Harvey

SKETCHUP PRO CONSULTANT - Patrick Kelly

The design of every space begins with a story, often spoken, but never untold. Narratives about design communicate more than any color, hue, texture, furniture element, style or theme. Design stories are stories about people—the users of the space, or the designer of the space, or some combination of both.

This book tells my story, but it also illustrates how a different view of color may help you to tell your own. I begin by sharing how I came to my insights about color and light, and then apply what I've learned by illustrating 16 unique approaches inspired by my travels around the globe. I will explain how and why each was chosen, and illustrate how lighting, both exterior and interior can complement a color palette, fulfilling the potential of any space.

YELLOW

RED

GREEN

BLUE

NATURE'S FOUR COLOR WHEEL

4

TABLE OF CONTENTS

FOREWORD

Architects and designers have struggled for centuries to master color and light. Few have achieved regular success. Color is hard.

The colors of built environments are prisoners of limited materials. Mother Nature's colors are unlimited, but change daily, seasonally, and with the movement of the sun. Color is deeply personal, rooted in our memories of people and places, and has a measureable impact on mood. From our earliest years wearing pastel pink or baby blue, we learn colors have cultural and societal meanings. And then we age, and our perception of color changes. Color is *really* hard.

Against seemingly insurmountable difficulties managing color in the face of taste, time, and market forces, some retreat. The flag of surrender is the "Navajo white" and "Bone" that permeates our apartments and tract homes, not to mention the Modern Movement. Today's automobiles are available in enough gray shades to drive Henry Ford mad, but strong colors are becoming rare. We admire the teal and white two-tone cars of yesteryear, but we do not run out to buy new cars in fierce colors (with the possible exception of "Fire Engine Red").

It's not surprising, then, that color is among the most difficult subjects to both teach and learn. Many design programs remove color from first assignments to help new students concentrate on geometry, shape, and form. There is much to understand about color, and knowledge gained comes from surprising sources. It does not take long before design students learn about Frank Lloyd Wright's beloved "Cherokee Red" or how Ricardo Legorreta and Steven Holl bounce daylight off vibrant colors to magical effect.

Designers are taught color perception- that light colors make rooms seem larger, that warm colors advance and cool colors recede. The 314-page *Color-aid* book was once a required tool in the design studio. Over time, monochromatic and complementary color schemes gave way to triadic, analogous, split-complementary, and other schemes Computers introduced new ways of understanding and communicating color including the disruptive discovery that the luminous colors on the screen do not match the results on the paper. We discovered aging has a significant impact on color perception, an important safety consideration in housing projects for the elderly.

Most design students graduate feeling that they do not understand color well. Things don't improve when they start practicing. In this book, Gloria Jaroff, AIA proposes a solution, using nature as the basis for color strategy. She is not the first to propose this idea. AIA Gold-Medal winner and noted design studio instructor Joseph Esherick used to say that he "does not use any color that cannot be found in a eucalyptus leaf." Designing color from nature is a strong idea, but is abstract putting into practice. We may marvel at the colors of fall leaves, the greens of a dark forest, and the muted colors of the desert—but then what? Gloria Jaroff has a suggestion: turn Esherick's abstraction into a tool. Observe and use the colors of your design project's natural environment. Don't just look at nature's colors, employ them. *The Nature of Color* considers contrast, color combination, backgrounds, and proportion to extract a color philosophy unique to each design. It's both a refreshing and practical approach.

We are reminded that nature's colors are not static hues and shades. We may see the exuberant colors of fall leaves, but are astonished when they lie on the ground, float on an icy stream - their colors reflected back in shiny surfaces, or sink to the bottom. Nature adds variety, *luminosity*, and depth that paint cannot match. For this, Jaroff helps us understand how *luminosity* is lost with chemical oxides in paint colors the same way flavor is lost when we breed tomatoes to better stand early harvest and longer travel.

Many books explore color in the built environment, but there should be more—many more. Color is hard and making color decisions risky. Color theories abound, but theory is an abstraction. Perhaps there's an easier way. Perhaps, as Jaroff points out in the following pages, the solution is all around us.

Douglas Noble, FAIA, Ph.D.

Karen M. Kensek, LEED AP [BD+C], Associate AIA

TO HARVEY
Whose photographs taught me to
COMPREHEND
And inspired this book.

TO JIM
Who taught me to LISTEN
And whose humor, playfulness and music
Are imbedded on every page.

Yosemite National Park's Half Dome is a symbol of strength and courage, and a place to rest and contemplate.

THE NATURE OF COLOR

in interior design

Gloria Jaroff, AIA

ACKNOWLEDGEMENTS

It's an impossible task to adequately thank or acknowledge the generosity and contributions of everyone who made this book possible. Above all, this book would not have happened without the technical support and encouragement of my nephew, Richard Buday, FAIA, who not only contributed endless hours of editing and rendering, but also believed in my story, holding my hand throughout the entire two and a half year process.

I thank also my son, Joe Jaroff and my daughter-in-law, Bhavani for their generosity and sharing, and whom I can always count on for support and inspiration. Special thanks to my friend, Dr. Barbara Marantz for editing the introduction and for her wonderful ear, and to my incredibly talented graphics team, Pinky Rose Job and Pedro Calixto, who embellished the computer models. Karen Wong's steadfast devotion and tiger energy magically turned my story into the book you're now reading.

I owe many thanks to Tom and Linda Buday, Michael Buday, Richard Buday, Reagan James, Mishone Feigin, Ryan Schiff, Elana Jaroff, Samuel Abraham, Joan Facer, Cassandra Tondro, Sandra Castleman and Sam Lubell for generously providing photographs. You'll find a treasure of great art hanging on the walls of the models thanks to the following artists: Bob Boreman, Gene Buday, Edison Crayne, Victoria Crayne, Doug Edge, Joshua Elias, Sylvia Greer, Arleen Hendler, Reagan James, Cinthia Joyce, Tom Lieber, Margaret Noesner, Carole Spence and Cassandra Tondro.

Additional thanks goes to other family members and friends for marketing tips, priceless feedback and moral support throughout the process: Tom Buday, Bob Buday, Catherine Buday, Saisha Grayson Knoth, Reagan James, Ryan Schiff, Edwin Paul, Ed and Victoria Crayne, Dennis Tanida, Bruce Schaffer, Virginia Lloyd, Elana Jaroff, Harper Jaroff, Lois Buday, Gene Buday, Joan Grantz, Caren Grantz Keljik, Mark Keljik, Bob Boreman, Bruce Schaffer, Trudy Armer, Mark Kaufman, John Kaufman, Juanda Christian, Zoe Koufopoulos, Peter Facer, Bill Megalos, Donal and J.S. Gibson, Frank Kurland, Jim Budman, Sylvia Greer, Andre Nawrocky, Sandra Price, Marv Harden, Jack Neworth, Arleen Hendler, Rosemary Parrish, Greg Dahl, Nino Fanali, Kathryn Creamer, Kenneth Vick, Connie Crothers, Gary Goldstein, Nancy Fulton, Ellen Baum, Ty Wapato—and last, but never least, Dish Taylor who helped retain my sanity and taught me the art of patience.

INTRODUCTION -WHY I WROTE THIS BOOK

THE DESIGN OF EVERY SPACE BEGINS WITH A STORY, OFTEN SPOKEN, BUT NEVER UNTOLD. DESIGN NARRATIVES COMMUNICATE MORE THAN ANY COLOR, HUE, TEXTURE, FURNITURE ELEMENT, STYLE OR THEME.

While employed by HNTB Architects under contract to Walt Disney Imagineering, I worked on theme park designs for Tokyo Disney Sea, Paris Second Gate and California Adventure. Surrounded by master storytellers, I soon learned how naturally designed details, including color and palette, fall into place—but only once a story is established.

I use this book not only to tell my story, but also to illustrate how a different view of color may help you to tell your own story. What follows is how I came to my insights about color and light, and then applied it to 16 unique design approaches inspired by my travels around the globe. I explain how and why each was chosen, and illustrate how lighting, both exterior and interior can complement a color palette, fulfilling the potential of a space.

Color is as fickle and unpredictable as the stock market. Color perception is affected by the unique lighting quality of its environment. Having lived and practiced, both design and architecture on two coasts, and with clients in the Midwest and Europe, I find it necessary to use different color palettes for every location.

No two people see colors exactly the same way due to varying degrees of eye health or color blindness, as well as cultural and emotional response. Stylistic trends and marketing strategies may also influence color palette choices. Color will change in a room depending on orientation (North, South, East, West), time of day, and season. Color also varies depending on the texture or finish of a surface or material.

If you have agonized over color chips in an effort to choose just the right wall color, or if you've tried to match and coordinate with an existing rug or other furnishing, or struggled to achieve a very specific feeling or look, you are not alone. You've been wrestling with the mystery of color, and probably over many years as I have —fifty years, in fact, practicing both interior design and architecture.

I've come to understand that simply using a color wheel as taught in design school or in design books (which may work for artists, graphic designers, or in advertising) does little to solve the complex problem of selecting the right commercial paint chip colors and applying them in a way that creates a built environment. I have found better ways to do that, and that is the purpose of this book.

This manual is my attempt to share with you my understanding of how color occurs in a particular environment. It also tells the story of how this insight evolved into a new way of understanding color, a fresh approach to applying color to design.

The *Jaroff Contrast Color System* is a way of using Mother Nature's four background colors—yellow, red, blue and green—as an additive system, and applying the idea to eight *Composite Color Wheels* as a subtractive system based on commercial house paints.

I have found dynamic interaction among complex natural forces working in a contrast system produces the *luminosity* we perceive as color. Applying these principles can simplify and enhance the process of color selection for interiors.

Each color scheme, using the *Jaroff Contrast Color System*, incorporates all visible colors. Combining all of light's perceived visible colors produces white (daylight), which is the standard for measuring artificial lighting. Incandescent and fluorescent lamps are rated combining both Kelvin (temperature) as an indication of how close the light is to daylight, and color rendering index (CRI) for how faithfully colors from the full spectrum are perceived on a scale from 0 to 100. New metrics are being created for today's emerging LED lighting systems.

The computer renderings in this book were modeled in Trimble Navigation Limited's SketchUp Pro and rendered with SU Podium V2 Plus. They are based on environmental photography from my personal journeys, with a little help on missing photos from my friends. I used my painter's eye to not only capture the feeling or essence of each landscape, but also to express my personal connection. In my design practice. Whether a project is commercial or residential, I have a client to share the creative journey with me. The dynamic relationship between client and designer brings together the client's intuitive understanding of what is desired with the designer's technical know-how. Together, we reach personally meaningful design solutions.

The models are pure fun, part fantasy and with some surprises thrown in. They should not be taken literally. Interestingly, all of the models are based on a single floor plan. It's amazing how many different ways one can interpret the design of a space, and how graphic representation saves money by comparing alternate schemes before investing in redesign.

Paint colors throughout the book are Color Preview from Benjamin Moore & Co., and were imported into Photoshop and SketchUp Pro not only as design elements in the models, but also as an aid in explaining how house paints are organized differently from artists' colors. You can order 8" x 8" color samples of any color by registering on the www.benjaminmoore.com website.

Disclaimers: All product and company names or numbers are trademarks™ or registered® trademarks of their respective holders. Use of them does not imply any affiliation with or endorsement by them.

Please note that any digital or electronic representation of any color is not 100% accurate, given the vagaries of color translation on computers monitors, digital devices or in print. As well, colors viewed online or in print will not reproduce exactly the same way when applied to a physical surface. Most paint stores will be able to reasonably match colors from this book. Check with your local paint store or Benjamin Moore technical support for proper materials for preparation, application and for specific finishes or products appropriate for your project.

THE STORY

MY JOURNEY WITH COLOR

THE STORY OF MY JOURNEY WITH COLOR

THE BEGINNING:
My search for inspiration

I began this book to describe how colors behave under varying degrees of light. I thought I would be drawing on my design education and 50 plus years experience as an architect and interior designer in residential and commercial projects. But I was in for a surprise.

Nature as inspiration for an interior:

Not long ago, on a family trip driving to New England, I saw Mother Nature in a way I had never seen her. Many design books suggest looking to nature for inspiration, but they don't say how. As I began really seeing and listening, I put aside my preconceived notions and book learning about design and started thinking (again) like an artist. I decided it might be fun to paint an interior as a work of art, combining a sense of light with the essence of a landscape or cityscape as inspiration. Now living in Southern California, but having grown up in the Northeast and traveling extensively, I had plenty to draw from.

OBSERVATIONS OF NATURE'S METHODS:
Contrast:

At first I noticed nature's use of contrast in four categories: value, color, movement and light. Contrasts were enormous in one landscape, muted and understated in others. Yet all had the same four basic elements of contrast. The way nature arranges opposites of values, colors, movement and light creates a special type of contrast called *luminosity*. Look around and you'll see the same things: dark versus light, rough versus smooth texture, large versus small, bright versus muted. The greatest degree of contrast, or lack of contrast, is often value, the difference between areas of light and dark.

Color combinations:

My next discovery was the constant play of a bright element supported by a neutral material. For example, bright green leaves are supported in nature by the muted earth tones of tree trunks and branches, mirroring the structural nature of the wood. The blues of the ocean are magnified by the yellow-beige tones of sand.

Backgrounds and Proportion:

I also noted the function of background elements (grass, trees, mountains, water, sky) were just that— support for brighter small elements, like colorful birds or spring flowers, blooming and then quickly dying. Recalling how fall foliage and brilliant sunsets last for a moment, I concluded that if Mother Nature uses these colors in small doses, the same techniques should apply to interiors.

THE MIDDLE:
Extracting a color philosophy from Nature - A Four Color System

As I looked deeper, comparing landscapes or cityscapes, I saw the repetition of the four distinct colors (yellow, red, blue and green) appearing in combinations in the largest areas or backgrounds. This led to the creation of the **Jaroff Contrast Color System**, a system of eight **Composite Color Wheels** organized around nature's recurring four background colors as perceived in light (an additive system).

Capturing Nature's Movement (Luminosity) in an Interior:

My next challenge was applying my philosophy to interior design by working with computer models. While I could apply my color observations to an organized set of color wheels, it wasn't enough. How do you express the deeper aspects of color that nature provides quite uniquely in the category of movement? Not only physical movement of wind, water, waves, clouds, birds and butterflies revealing a kaleidoscopic view of color, but also a kind of music. There are sounds of waves crashing, water rippling, rain falling, birds singing, and foghorns. There are also odors of grass after a rainfall, pine needles in a forest or the salt air of the ocean. That movement, as it relates to color and light is an integral part of *luminosity*. Consider how many shades of green are viewable in a single leaf, and then multiply that by the movement of wind and changes in light from morning to evening or one season to another. Or, consider the blue and green waters of a windswept ocean and the sounds of water lapping on sand with the sun reflecting sparkling light on each wave.

In the past (even as recently as 20 and 30 years ago) some of this *luminosity* was captured in Oriental rug weaving by a process called "abrash". The fibers were not dyed in one batch creating variation in the colors amongst the batches. This resulted in a variation in the bands across the rug as it was woven in horizontal rows producing an animated rainbow of color combinations. Fabrics like Emperor's Garden (J.H.Thorpe Co) used 16 screens to produce a product more like a Renaissance painting than decorative fabric.

During the 1950's and 60's I worked occasionally with a contractor who mixed his own paints from artists' pigments such as burnt sienna, raw sienna, yellow ochre raw umber and burnt umber. The resulting large painted expanses of wall were luminous, revealing a depth of layers and subtle undertones from the pigments used in the mixing. Today most paints are mixed with chemical oxides, which improve their ultra violet resistance, but at the expense of *luminosity*. In many ways much has been lost. Almost everything we now produce seems flat. Flooring and fabric fibers are dyed in solution resulting in uniformity, but lifeless color. Finely crafted custom furnishings with luminous wood graining with the depth and nobility of patina are a rarity.

The sparkle of nature that comes from the movement of time and elements is not directly translatable into an interior, but it is essential to the soul. Since many luminous products are no longer available, the challenge is finding a way to design using all of one's senses. This requires substituting a different kind of movement to replace Mother Nature's time and weather elements, and the dearth of luminous furnishings.

Re-organization of the color system around "afterimage"

As I began to apply my color philosophy to these models I realized the most successful palettes included *masstones* or *undertones* of all four of nature's yellow, red, blue and green. In that sense they were all complementary color palettes, whether high or low contrast. I use the basic definition of a complementary hue as its *afterimage*. You can check this out for yourself with the following experiment: close your eyes and cover them with your hands in the presence of any light source (outdoors works best). Most often you will see blues and greens. When you release your hands (keeping your eyes closed) you will see the opposite colors, yellows and reds, which are *afterimages* of the original colors.

The phenomenon of *afterimage* reinforced my philosophy of the **Jaroff Contrast Color System.** I reorganized the **Composite Color Wheel** (originally arranged with a single color in each of four quadrants), turning the wheel 1/8 turn counterclockwise, thereby placing two colors sharing the same *undertones* in each quadrant. Complementary (*afterimage*) colors were arranged directly opposite each other on the **Composite Color Wheel.** Quadrants could be combined from one **Composite Color Wheel** to another, intermixing Sun Colors, Mineral Colors, Earth Tones or Off Whites. I renamed each color to include the *masstone* and *undertone*, as well as temperature (warm or cool). For example, in the shared yellow and green quadrant in the **Cool Earth Tone Color Wheel,** the color names are: *Yellow/Green/C and Green/Yellow/C.* (Page 60, 61)

The Power Palette Concept:

I have found reproducing the essence of *luminosity* in a scene with paint color alone an exercise in futility. Understanding that interior environments are static is the best way to accept that selecting one color is never too important. It is always the palette or combination of colors, textures, lighting, values (and most of all, employing some type of movement) that captures the essence of a scene, breathing life into (animating) an interior environment.

My reason for creating the three-dimensional models in this book was to recreate a sense of movement through contrast (high or low)—with judicious proportions and placement of colors and textures—to either move or rest the eye and the body. I tried to capture the essence of each scene, much like improvising on a jazz tune. Some of the models mirror the color proportions of the scene. Others reverse the order of support and focus. I often began with one approach and changed direction in the middle, allowing each model to tell me what it wanted to be (thank you Louis Kahn). The resulting **JCCS Undertone Color Wheels** are combinations of **JCCS Composite Color Wheels** and a simplified guide mirroring color combinations as I perceived them in nature.

THE END:
How it all came together and worked in the production of 16 three-dimensional computer models.

If the major hue in a landscape was a *Blue/Green/W,* most of the time it was balanced in the model with a *Red/Yellow/W* or a *Yellow/Red/C* tone from the same chromatic wheel or another. Blue with a red *undertone* from the **Mineral Composite Color Wheel** balanced perfectly with a *Yellow/Green* from **Earth Tone Composite Color Wheel**. Greens with a yellow *undertone* from **Earth Tone** and **Sun Composite Color Wheels** were balanced by selecting a red with a blue *undertone* from the **Earth Tone Composite Color Wheel**. In other words, it seemed that the most complete models included all four of the yellow, red, blue or green colors. The final challenge was lighting each interior and illustrating the exterior lighting conditions that determined the choice of color palette as it related to each geographic area.

A bonus:

In the process of researching for photographs and images, there were serendipitous connections with a journalist from Paris, a web radio station in Barcelona, Spain, and a mural company in Rixheim, France. The final bonus has been revisiting memories of each area that tell the story of my personal connection, not only to each site, but to Mother Nature in general, and to deepening connections with family, friends, and whatever higher power has guided me.

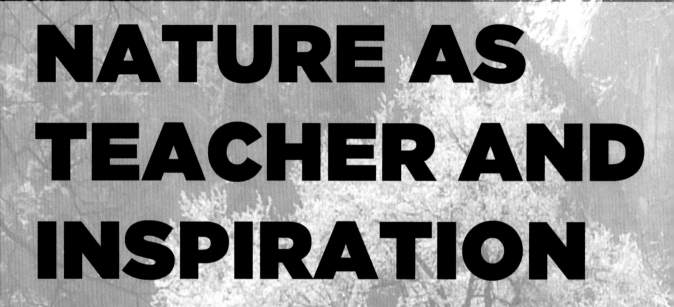

NATURE AS TEACHER AND INSPIRATION

THE FOUR COLORS IN NATURE // THE FOUR ELEMENTS OF CONTRAST

PART ONE

BLUES
IN NATURE

GREENS
IN NATURE

REDS
IN NATURE

YELLOWS
IN NATURE

Contrast:

Contrasts are enormous in one landscape and quite muted and understated in another.

The Concept of Contrast in Nature
Which side of the equation is yours?

Technically, contrast is the difference in brightness separating an object from its background. Because we each have a unique sensitivity to that brightness our color choices and palette preferences will be either high contrast or low contrast. The interior models in Part Four represent both concepts.

LOW CONTRAST*

*Low Contrast: McClaren Pond watercolor, © Edison T. Crayne

HIGH CONTRAST**

** High Contrast: DE4 oil on canvas, © Doug Edge

What is your Contrast Palette preference?

Nature's Four Basic Elements of Contrast
value, color, movement, and light.

LOW CONTRAST

VALUE CONTRAST: LOW
Light to Medium Values

COLOR CONTRAST: LOW
Subdued

LIGHTING CONTRAST: LOW
Hazy, reflected light only, minimizing
contrast between backgrounds

MOVEMENT: LOW - Horizontal

IMPLIED MOVEMENT: birds, boats,
wind, fog, precipitation, seasonal
changes.

HIGH CONTRAST

VALUE CONTRAST: HIGH
Light, Medium and Dark Values

COLOR CONTRAST: HIGH
Intense, Sun Colors/Earth Tones

LIGHTING CONTRAST: HIGH
Strong sunlight with both direct and
reflected light. Sparkle of the sun reflecting on the white- capped waves.

MOVEMENT: HIGH - Multi-directional

IMPLIED MOVEMENT: birds, high
winds, crashing waves and tidal
changes.

Value Contrast:

The greatest degree of contrast is often value, the difference between large areas of light compared with large areas of dark.

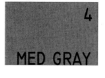

Value Contrast: HIGH
(light, medium and dark)

Value Contrast: LOW
(light to medium gray)

W   **G/B**   **C**

2029-10   2121-30

Color Contrast:

Bright elements supported by a neutral material.

Bright green leaves supported by muted earth tones of tree trunks and branches (mirroring the structural nature of the wood).

W

2062-40   2106-60

The rich blue/greens of the ocean and sky magnified by the yellow/red beige tones of the sand.

Movement in Nature
Luminosity:

The sparkle of nature that results from the movement of time and the elements is not directly translatable into an interior, but it is to the soul. The challenge is to find a way to design using all your senses, substituting a different kind of movement to replace nature's time and weather elements.

Physical movement of wind, water, waves, clouds, birds and butterflies reveals a kaleidoscopic view of color, accompanied by a symphony of sounds.

Imagine the music of waves crashing, water rippling, rain falling, birds singing and the odors of grass after a rainfall, pine needles in a forest or the salt air of the ocean.

Many shades of green are viewable in a single leaf, multiplied by the movement of wind and changes in light from morning to evening and one season to another. Variations can be found in value, color and depth from the top sunlit portion of a tree branch reflecting the moving shadows of the leaves, compared with the dark underneath part hidden from the sun and totally in shade.

Consider the sounds of water lapping on the sand with the sun reflecting a sparkling light on each wave.

Movement in Interiors
Luminosity:

Emperor's Garden a sixteen-screen hand-blocked print, glowing with Renaissance-like painted detail.

J.H. Thorpe
Company

Luminosity was captured in Oriental rug weaving by a process called "abrash." Fibers were not dyed in a single batch, which created variation in the colors among the batches. This resulted in differences in the bands across the rug as it was woven in horizontal rows, ultimately producing an animated rainbow of color combinations.

Mark Keljik, Keljik's Oriental Rugs, Minneapolis, MN

Similar naturally occurring variations can be found in parquet wood flooring and finely crafted furnishings with rich leather and luminous wood graining.

Eames Lounge Chair and Ottoman
Eames Bent Plywood Chair and Walnut Stool
Courtesy of Herman Miller Inc.

The Language of Color, Light and Vision

**COLOR IS DEPENDENT ON A LIGHT SOURCE STRIKING REFLECTIVE SURFACES,
BUT PERCEPTION OF COLOR IS A SUBJECTIVE PSYCHOLOGICAL PHENONMENON OF THE BRAIN**

THE SOURCE OF LIGHT:
The sun (or artificial luminaire) as a direct light source, projects wavelengths in the visible spectrum that are assigned the color properties of red, yellow, green, and blue.

Color is not a property of a wavelength, which has only length, frequency and amplitude.

Rainbows show color in the visible spectrum, from red to yellow to green to blue. The mixture of the entire spectrum of visible light forms the perception of white light.

VISION THE SOURCE OF COLOR:
Color is a complex mechanism, from the retinal cone cells in our eyes to the visual cortex in the brain, which allows us to interpret a light wave as color.

MOST LIGHT IS REFLECTED:
Some light is direct from the sun, producing highlights and shadows, but most light is indirect or reflected.

When light energy reaches a surface, light waves can be selectively absorbed as heat, transmitted by passing through a transparent surface, or reflected in either a diffuse (multidirectional) or specular manner (bouncing off smooth or opaque surfaces).

EXTERIOR REFLECTED LIGHT:
Reflecting surfaces on the right are the ocean, reflecting the blue green color of the sky, and sand, reflecting the yellow/red *afterimage* colors.

The image on the left shows highlights and shadows in both direct and indirect light. Leaves and grass are absorbing red/blue and reflect green/yellow. The tree trunks and wood siding are reflecting the red/blue *afterimage* colors of the foliage.

A blue sky is the result of air molecules scattering (reflecting) the sun's shortest wavelengths, which are scattered more strongly than the longer red wavelengths.

Exterior Lighting Contrast

ALL STORIES ARE REVEALED THROUGH COLOR AND LIGHTING CONTRAST

LIGHTING CONTRAST: LOW

A cloudy day with no direct sunlight and no shadow creates little contrast.
All light is indirect or reflected.

LIGHT COLOR: Surrounding elements are colored with the gray/blues of the ocean reflected from the sky. Interior painted surfaces will take on a bluish gray tone. Bright colors may appear garish.

LIGHTING CONTRAST: HIGH

The sun is illuminating the contrast between wood, rocks, leaves and grass, creating strong highlights and deep shadows, as well as areas of indirect or reflected light.

LIGHT COLOR: Deep greens reflected from the landscape alter the color perception of large painted interior surfaces.

Interior Lighting Contrast

A WELL DESIGNED INTERIOR LIGHTING PLAN CAN CREATE AN EMOTIONAL IMPACT AND SUPPORT THE STORY OR MOOD BY CONTROLLING THE DEGREE OF LUMINANCE CONTRAST, OR STIMULATION. IT SHOULD ALSO HIGHLIGHT DESIGN ELEMENTS AND REINFORCE THE INTENDED ACTIVITY OF THE SPACE .

LIGHTING TECHNIQUES*

High contrast/low contrast spaces are created by manipulating the relationship of lighted surfaces (focus or foreground) to those in comparative darkness (surround or background).

Direct and indirect light fixtures can be combined to create ambient light, focus, and fill for highlighting artwork, sparkle to create drama, and grazing techniques for stone and other textures.

DESIGN CONSIDERATIONS:

The apparent size of a space will be affected by glazing types: (size, placement and type of windows, doors, skylights), furniture layout and ceiling height.

EXTERIOR CONSIDERATIONS:
**Geographic Location and
Sun Orientation of the space:
(North, South, East, West)**

In the Southern climates with bright sunlight, the iris of the eye contracts, limiting light reaching the retina and permitting more intense Sun Colors to be viewed comfortably. In the Northern hemisphere, the iris expands allowing more light to enter the eye. Softer Mineral Colors and Earth Tones are easier to tolerate in expansive areas.

LIGHTING CONTRAST: LOW

This image shows a large amount of diffuse or indirect/ambient light, and only a small amount of focused/direct light.

DEGREE OF STIMULATION:** Minimal chromatic contrast, similar to the quality of an overcast day.

EMOTIONAL IMPACT:** Finishes appear flat and equal. Individual reactions range from relaxation and comfort to neutral and boring.

VALUE AND FINISHES: Large surfaces with higher light reflectance values (LRV), Earth Tones and Off Whites reflect more light and increase the apparent size of the space. Light smooth or polished surfaces increase inter-reflection of light between surfaces filling shadows, reducing contrast and creating a higher luminance or more uniform light with a low contrast appearance.

Season of the Year: The angle of the sun is lower in winter allowing more daylight to enter.

Time of Day: Light tends to appear warmer at sunrise and sunset, and more white at noon.

Note: The colors for each model were chosen to reflect the type of exterior lighting unique to that geographic area. A brighter palette was chosen for the red light of the Sedona model. In the Connecticut model, softer colors are predominant in large areas and bright colors used for accents.

*Note: The technical aspects of lighting an interior cannot be covered thoroughly in this book and are best studied in other sources on the subject. The summaries and contrast comparisons on pages 40-43 list general guidelines and issues to consider for residential lighting.

Interior Lighting Contrast

LUMINANCE (PERCEIVED BRIGHTNESS) IS THE SUM TOTAL OF LIGHT — DIRECT AND INDIRECT — STRIKING ALL SURFACES, COMBINED WITH THE PROPERTIES (SIZE, COLOR AND TEXTURE) OF THOSE SURFACES THAT ALLOW TRANSMISSION OR REFLECTION AS EITHER DIFFUSE OR SPECULAR LIGHT

INTERIOR REFLECTED LIGHT:
Any object that reflects or transmits light is a secondary light source. The larger the surface, the more light and color will be reflected onto other objects and surfaces in the space.

In the room on the left, light is transmitted through glass, interior reflections and inter-reflections. Colored light is exchanged between walls, ceiling, flooring and furniture, reinforcing the overall gray/blue color palette contrasted with warm accents.

LIGHTING CONTRAST: HIGH
This image shows a large amount of focused, direct light. Bright highlights and crisp shadows create deep contrast between foreground and background. Focus and emphasis is achieved in some areas, with relative darkness in others.

The image has a small amount of diffuse ambient light. Sparkle is used for concentrated accent lighting.

DEGREE OF STIMULATION: The image shows increased stimulation and activity. It's energetic, like a sunny day.

EMOTIONAL IMPACT: The image shows how lighting can create liveliness, alertness, direct attention, hold interest, produce focus, drama, and visual excitement to highlight texture and detail.

VALUE AND FINISHES: Dark colors (low LRV values) and highly textured finishes (wood 10-50% or granite 20-25%) absorb more light and have lower reflectance properties than polished surfaces (metal 60-80%).

LAMPING:
Since paint colors and dyed materials may match under some lighting , but not others (a phenomenon called metamerism), it is important to check finishes with alternate lamps that have both the correct temperature and minimum 90 color rendering index (CRI) for good color matching.

LED bulbs should be evaluated on an individual basis until more advanced metrics are established in this fast evolving technology.

CONTROL SYSTEMS:
Light fixtures with diffusers or filters, window coverings, shading techniques and lighting control systems can be used to control mood and lighting levels, brightness ratios, and glare, as well as reduce environmental load.

**Note: Individual responses to lighting contrast, like color, are purely subjective and not universal in nature.

Backgrounds and Proportion

Nature uses grass, trees, mountains, water, and sky to support brighter elements, like colorful flowers that bloom and then quickly die.

Fall foliage and brilliant sunsets last for a moment. Since nature uses these intense colors in small doses, the same technique can be applied to interiors.

THE MIDDLE:

Part Two - Extracting a Color Philosophy from Nature - the *Jaroff Contrast Color System (JCCS)*

The repetition of four distinct *masstones* in nature's backgrounds underpins the **JCCS Contrast Color Wheel**, a system of **Eight Composite Color Wheels** incorporating nature's four *masstones/ undertones* yellow, red, blue and green organized around *afterimage.*

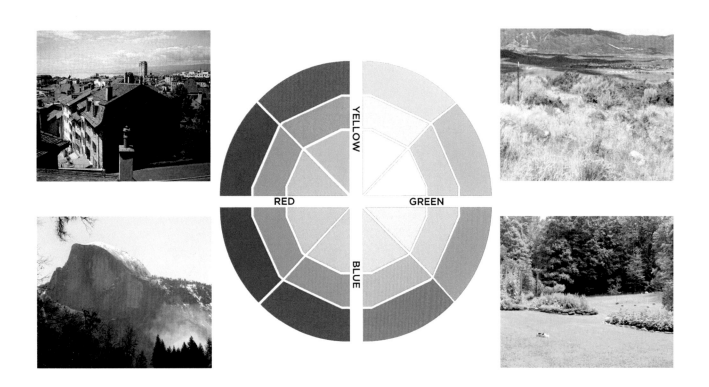

DESIGNING A NEW FOUR COLOR SYSTEM

THE FOUR STEPS

PART TWO

STEP ONE: DESIGNING A DIFFERENT COLOR WHEEL

A color wheel is an instrument to support a color principle or philosophy. Hues are illustrated counterclockwise in a circle to simulate the order in which they are perceived in the visible light color spectrum.

NATURE'S FOUR COLOR WHEEL
The *Jaroff Contrast Color System (JCCS)*

JCCS is organized around four colors in an additive light system. It's adapted to commercial paints for selecting colors for building substrates: walls, furnishings or exteriors. Hues from the *JCCS Color Wheels* can also be used for matching wall colors to existing fabrics and furnishings.

The four colors are yellow, red, blue and green as derived from nature's backgrounds of grass, leaves, water, sky, wood, earth, rocks and sand. Because it's an additive system, all colors when combined produce white. The ideal of sunlight at high noon and white light are standards against which our artificial lighting sources are measured.

Tints and shades in commercial paints are mixed differently from artists' pigments.

Note: All colors are based on Benjamin Moore Color Preview paints. Every effort has been made to ensure accuracy of color information, however colors in print and online may not reproduce accurately and can only approximate the color and finish of an actual paint. Use Benjamin Moore color chips or larger samples from their website, www.benjaminmoore.com when making a color selection.

THE ARTISTS' 12 COLOR WHEEL

A standard artists' color wheel is based on three primary colors (yellow, red and blue), 3 secondary colors and 6 tertiary colors, and is used as a guide for mixing pigments for paper, canvas or other media. The purpose is creating fine art or advertising.

An artists' color wheel is a subtractive system, because all pigments when mixed together produce black. With each addition of pigment, more color is subtracted (absorbed) and less color (or light) is reflected. White is added to artists' pigments to tint or lighten a color. Black is added to darken or produce a shade.

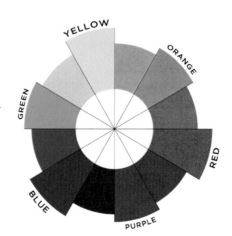

STEP TWO: OBSERVING FOUR ASPECTS OF NATURE'S FOUR COLORS
with house paints on a color wheel

1. THE VALUE ASPECT -
Dark, Medium, and Light.

Value is measured by light reflectance value, (LRV). The Grayscale photo below can be used to compare each color (hue) with its corresponding value component on the *JCCS Color Wheel.* *

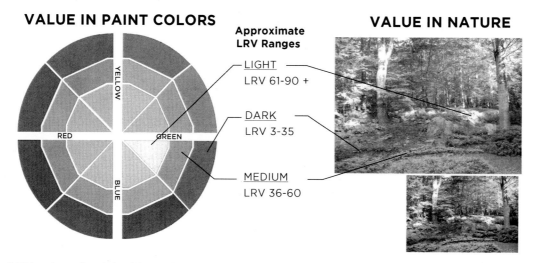

VALUE IN PAINT COLORS

Approximate LRV Ranges

LIGHT
LRV 61-90 +

DARK
LRV 3-35

MEDIUM
LRV 36-60

VALUE IN NATURE

LRV values furnished by paint companies for each color chip indicate the anticipated amount of light and heat absorbed or reflected from a surface painted with that color. A high LRV of 80 indicates the color will reflect 80% light from the surface and, therefore, absorb 20%, resulting in a light/cool space. Light, glossy smooth surfaces have high reflectance values. Rough textures tend to appear darker since they absorb more light.

Identifying the value aspect of a scene or color is more important than the hue itself. It is the key to defining the mood (low or high contrast)

2. TEMPERATURE
Warm and Cool

JCCS WARM COLOR WHEEL
(RED BASE)

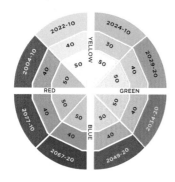

Some warm commercial paint colors are mixed with a red base, which is noted on a color chip with a "W."

JCCS COOL COLOR WHEEL
(BLUE BASE)

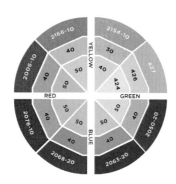

Some cool commercial paint colors are mixed with a blue base, noted on color chips with a "C."

3. CHROMATIC INTENSITY (SATURATION)
Bright and Muted (Toned)

THESE GREENS ARE BRIGHT (SATURATED)

THESE GREENS ARE MUTED (TONED)

This green is bright, dark and warm.

These greens appear light and have a warm yellow component, or *undertone*.

These greens are less saturated (less intense) and cooler.

THESE BLUES ARE BRIGHT (SATURATED)

THESE BLUES ARE MUTED (TONED)

These blues have strong red *undertones* and a high degree of Value contrast with the surrounding sky and trees.

These blues have strong green *undertones*.

These blues are more muted.

4. UNDERTONE

Each color has a *masstone* of yellow, red, blue or green and an *undertone* that defines its relationship to the adjacent color on the *JCCS Color Wheel.*

**THESE GREENS HAVE
A YELLOW *UNDERTONE***

**THESE GREENS HAVE
A YELLOW *UNDERTONE***

**THESE GREENS HAVE
A BLUE *UNDERTONE***

**THESE BLUES HAVE
A RED *UNDERTONE***

**THESE BLUES HAVE
A GREEN *UNDERTONE***

STEP THREE: COMPOSITE COLORS
Reorganization of the *Jaroff Contrast Color Wheel* around *afterimage*

To understand *afterimage*, try the following experiment: close your eyes and cover them with your hands in the presence of any light source. Outdoors works best. Most often you will see blues and greens. When you release your hands while keeping your eyes closed, you will see the opposite colors of yellow and red, which are *afterimage*s of the original colors.

The *afterimage* phenomenon reinforced my philosophy of a four-color system. Since *undertones* are more easily understood when viewed in the context of adjacent colors, I reorganized the original **JCCS Color Wheel**, rotating quadrants 1/8 turn counterclockwise so that each quadrant contained two colors sharing related *undertones*. True *afterimage* colors seemed to be automatically arranged directly opposite each other on the revised **JCCS Color Wheel**.

I then renamed each hue as a **JCCS Composite Color** to include its *masstone* and *undertone*, as well as its temperature (warm or cool). (See facing page)

A COLOR WHEEL BASED ON *JCCS COMPOSITE COLORS*
MASS TONES AND UNDERTONES

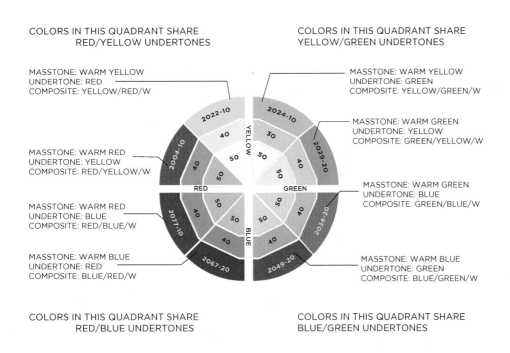

COLORS IN THIS QUADRANT SHARE
RED/YELLOW UNDERTONES

COLORS IN THIS QUADRANT SHARE
YELLOW/GREEN UNDERTONES

MASSTONE: WARM YELLOW
UNDERTONE: RED
COMPOSITE: YELLOW/RED/W

MASSTONE: WARM YELLOW
UNDERTONE: GREEN
COMPOSITE: YELLOW/GREEN/W

MASSTONE: WARM GREEN
UNDERTONE: YELLOW
COMPOSITE: GREEN/YELLOW/W

MASSTONE: WARM RED
UNDERTONE: YELLOW
COMPOSITE: RED/YELLOW/W

MASSTONE: WARM GREEN
UNDERTONE: BLUE
COMPOSITE: GREEN/BLUE/W

MASSTONE: WARM RED
UNDERTONE: BLUE
COMPOSITE: RED/BLUE/W

MASSTONE: WARM BLUE
UNDERTONE: RED
COMPOSITE: BLUE/RED/W

MASSTONE: WARM BLUE
UNDERTONE: GREEN
COMPOSITE: BLUE/GREEN/W

COLORS IN THIS QUADRANT SHARE
RED/BLUE UNDERTONES

COLORS IN THIS QUADRANT SHARE
BLUE/GREEN UNDERTONES

Note: A cool red with a blue undertone will appear cooler than a warm red with a blue undertone.

Undertones are more obvious in high intensity Sun or Mineral Colors. As colors are mixed and become less saturated Earth Tones and Off Whites they become less pure, making it difficult to detect *undertones* in an isolated color chip.

For matching and combining colors, recognizing *undertones* can make all the difference between a successful color palette and one that misses. If you are viewing Earth Tones in small color chips they may appear to have one *undertone*, but often reveal something different when painted on a large area. Checking a larger sample and comparing with other colors and materials in the palette will reveal whether the *undertones* are compatible or clash. Since Earth Tones are complex mixtures of many hues, *undertone* interpretations may vary and should also be checked under local lighting conditions (both interior and exterior) and on every surface.

JCCS WARM COMPOSITE COLOR WHEEL

1A WARM SUN COLOR WHEEL
(RED BASE)

1. Values:
   Medium to Low
2. Temp: Warm
3. Intensity: Medium
4. *Masstone:* Yellow
   Undertone: Green

1. Values:
   Medium to High
2. Temp: Warm
3. Intensity: High
4. *Masstone:* Green
   Undertone: Yellow

1. Values:
   Medium to High
2. Temp: Warm
3. Intensity: High
4. *Masstone:* Red
   Undertone: Yellow

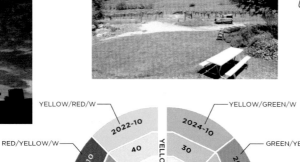

1. Values:
   Medium to High
2. Temp: Warm
3. Intensity: High
4. *Masstone:* Blue
   Undertone: Red

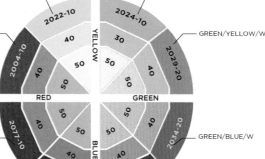

1. Values:
   Low to High
2. Temp: Warm
3. Intensity: High
4. *Masstone:* Blue
   Undertone:
   Green

JCCS COOL COMPOSITE COLOR WHEEL

2A COOL SUN COLOR WHEEL
(BLUE BASE)

1. Values:
   Medium to Dark
2. Temp: Cool
3. Intensity: Medium
4. *Masstone*: Red
   Undertone: Yellow

1. Values:
   Medium to Low
2. Temp: Cool
3. Intensity: Medium
4. *Masstone*: Yellow
   Undertone: Green

1. Values:
   Medium to Low
2. Temp: Cool
3. Intensity: Low
4. *Masstone*: Blue
   Undertone: Green

1. Values:
   Medium to Dark
2. Temp: Cool
3. Intensity: Low
4. Water *Masstone*: Red
   Undertone: Yellow
   Sky *Masstone*: Blue
   Undertone: Green

1. Values:
   Medium to Dark
2. Temp: Cool
3. Intensity: Low
4. *Masstone*: Green
   Undertone: Blue

STEP FOUR: The *JAROFF CONTRAST COLOR SYSTEM*
The Complete Color Wheel Story and How it Works

1. There are only four basic colors, or *masstones*, in nature's universe: yellow, red, blue and green.

2. Each *masstone* has a warm and a cool component.

3. Each color can be described as a *masstone* (the color immediately apparent on top) and/or an *undertone* (the concealed color that brings it closer to its adjacent color in the same quadrant of the *JCCS Color Wheel*).

4. Each *JCCS Composite Color* is a combination of a *masstone* and an *undertone*.

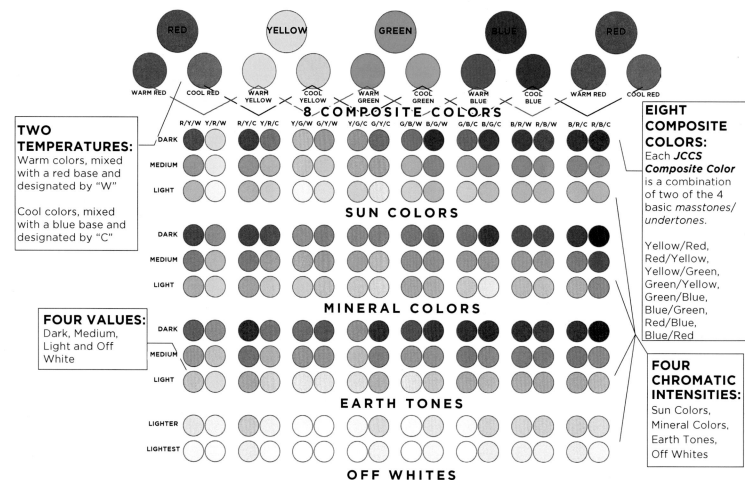

TWO TEMPERATURES:
Warm colors, mixed with a red base and designated by "W"

Cool colors, mixed with a blue base and designated by "C"

EIGHT COMPOSITE COLORS:
Each *JCCS Composite Color* is a combination of two of the 4 basic *masstones/undertones*.

Yellow/Red,
Red/Yellow,
Yellow/Green,
Green/Yellow,
Green/Blue,
Blue/Green,
Red/Blue,
Blue/Red

FOUR VALUES:
Dark, Medium, Light and Off White

FOUR CHROMATIC INTENSITIES:
Sun Colors,
Mineral Colors,
Earth Tones,
Off Whites

8 COMPOSITE COLORS

SUN COLORS

MINERAL COLORS

EARTH TONES

OFF WHITES

THE COMPLETE JCCS COLOR WHEEL STORY
EIGHT COMPOSITE COLOR WHEELS

Four Warm Composite Wheels and Four Cool Composite Wheels

Each color wheel is organized around nature's four *masstones* and *undertones* (yellow, red, blue and green) and the four aspects of color: temperature, value, chromatic intensity, and *undertone*.

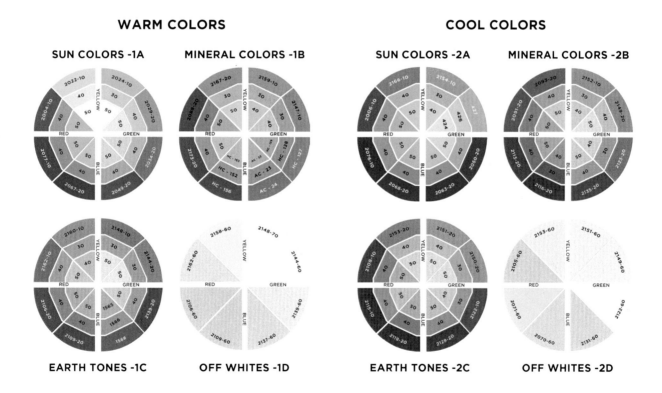

WARM COLORS

COOL COLORS

SUN COLORS -1A   MINERAL COLORS -1B   SUN COLORS -2A   MINERAL COLORS -2B

EARTH TONES -1C   OFF WHITES -1D   EARTH TONES -2C   OFF WHITES -2D

Note: The Composite Color Wheels have been organized as a guide. Not every color represented is recommended for use in an interior but is illustrated as a general guide and new approach to understanding undertones. Individual interpretations of undertones in a single paint chip will vary and are also influenced by the number of pigments in a paint, adjacent colors and examination of colors under varying light sources, both natural and artificial.

*Note: While there are ten gradations from black to white in a true value scale, the four values in this book (Dark, Medium, Light and Off White) are noted for clarification of the masstones chosen for practical interior application of **the JCCS Color Wheels**.

JCCS WARM COMPOSITE COLOR WHEELS

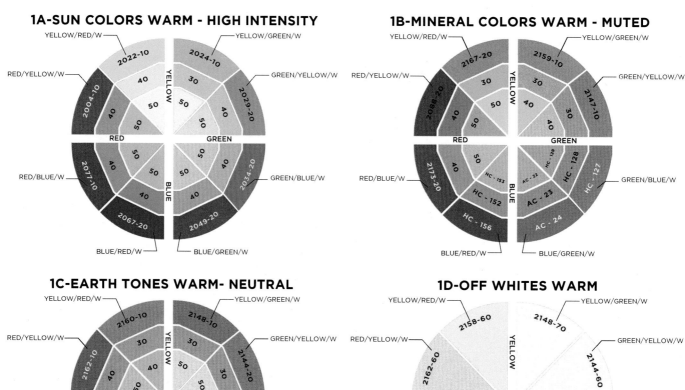

1A-SUN COLORS WARM - HIGH INTENSITY

1B-MINERAL COLORS WARM - MUTED

1C-EARTH TONES WARM- NEUTRAL

1D-OFF WHITES WARM

VALUES: OUTER CIRCLE - DARK   MIDDLE CIRCLE - MEDIUM   INNER CIRCLE - LIGHTEST

*Note: Every effort has been made to reasonably represent the Benjamin Moore Color Preview paints illustrated in the **JCCS Color Wheels**. However, since colors in print and online can only approximate the color and finish of a color chip, they are not to be considered accurate enough for exact color matching. For true color matching it is recommended that you obtain actual color chips from your local paint store or order large samples from their website, www.benjaminmoore.com*

JCCS COOL COMPOSITE COLOR WHEELS

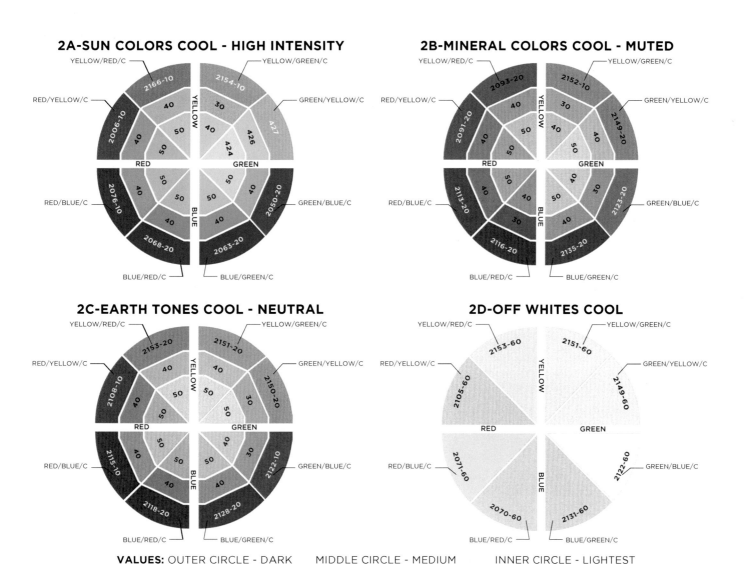

2A-SUN COLORS COOL - HIGH INTENSITY

YELLOW/RED/C — 2166-10
RED/YELLOW/C — 2006-10
YELLOW/GREEN/C — 2154-10
GREEN/YELLOW/C — 427
YELLOW — 40, 30, 40, 50, 50, 426, 424
GREEN — 50, 50, 40, 50, 40, 40
RED — 40, 50
RED/BLUE/C — 2076-10
GREEN/BLUE/C — 2050-20
BLUE — 50, 40
BLUE/RED/C — 2068-20
BLUE/GREEN/C — 2063-20

2B-MINERAL COLORS COOL - MUTED

YELLOW/RED/C — 2093-20
RED/YELLOW/C — 2091-20
YELLOW/GREEN/C — 2152-10
GREEN/YELLOW/C — 2149-20
YELLOW — 40, 30, 40, 50, 40
RED — 40, 50
RED/BLUE/C — 2113-20
GREEN/BLUE/C — 2123-20
BLUE — 50, 40, 40, 30, 50, 30
BLUE/RED/C — 2116-20
BLUE/GREEN/C — 2135-20

2C-EARTH TONES COOL - NEUTRAL

YELLOW/RED/C — 2153-20
RED/YELLOW/C — 2108-10
YELLOW/GREEN/C — 2151-20
GREEN/YELLOW/C — 2150-20
YELLOW — 40, 40, 50, 50, 30, 50
RED — 40, 50
RED/BLUE/C — 2115-10
GREEN/BLUE/C — 2122-10
BLUE — 50, 40, 50, 40, 50, 30, 40
BLUE/RED/C — 2118-20
BLUE/GREEN/C — 2128-20

2D-OFF WHITES COOL

YELLOW/RED/C — 2153-60
RED/YELLOW/C — 2105-60
YELLOW/GREEN/C — 2151-60
GREEN/YELLOW/C — 2149-60
YELLOW
GREEN
RED
RED/BLUE/C — 2071-60
GREEN/BLUE/C — 2122-60
BLUE
BLUE/RED/C — 2070-60
BLUE/GREEN/C — 2131-60

VALUES: OUTER CIRCLE - DARK   MIDDLE CIRCLE - MEDIUM   INNER CIRCLE - LIGHTEST

Colors in combination with other colors and materials will draw out different undertones of each color. Always check paint colors using large samples on every wall elevation and in varying lighting conditions in the area to be painted. Check paint samples with adjacent materials to verify matching for desired outcome under varying conditions. Color matching results will vary depending on texture, finish, lighting conditions, lighting fixtures and lamps.

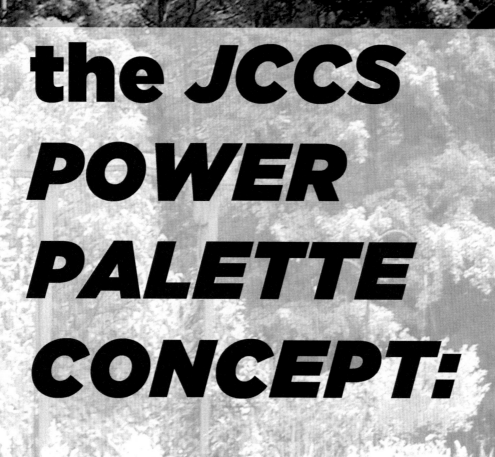

the *JCCS POWER PALETTE CONCEPT:*

CAPTURING THE ESSENCE OF NATURE'S LUMINOSITY

PART THREE

PART THREE - the *JCCS POWER PALETTE CONCEPT:*

IT'S NOT THE COLOR — IT'S THE CONTRAST

NATURE'S POWER PALETTES ARE BUILT ON CONTRAST

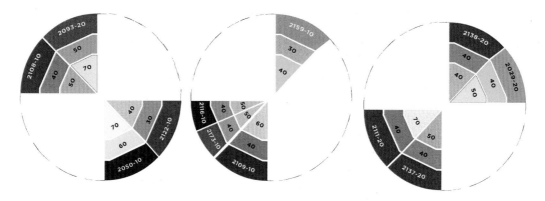

As I began to apply my color philosophy to three-dimensional models I realized the most successful palettes, whether high or low contrast, included *masstones* or *undertones* of all four of nature's colors yellow, red, blue and green), thus reinforcing the *afterimage* concept.

Since *afterimage* colors are automatically arranged directly opposite each other on *JCCS Composite Color Wheels*, colors from similar quadrants on any *JCCS Color Wheel* can easily be selected, combining Sun Colors, Mineral Colors, Earth Tones or Off Whites to create your own unique *JCCS Power Palette.*

For example, in the shared yellow and green quadrant of the *JCCS Cool Earth Tone Color Wheel,* the color names are: Yellow/Green/C and Green/Yellow/C. These can be combined with the Red/Blue/W of the *JCCS Mineral Color Wheel* or the Blue/Red/C of the *JCCS Sun Color Wheel* to produce a combined, unique *JCCS Undertone Color Wheel*. This simplifies the selection of paints to achieve a successful color scheme.

Capturing *Luminosity* in Interiors
Adapting nature's movement and light to interior design

I have found that reproducing the essence of *luminosity* in a scene with paint color alone an exercise in futility. Understanding that interior environments are static is the best way to accept selecting one color is never too important. It's always the palette or combination of colors, textures, lighting, values and movement that captures the essence of a scene and breathes life into (animates) an interior environment.

MOVEMENT IN INTERIORS

Nature's movement is not directly translatable to interior environments, but can be implied by focusing on contrast using:

Artwork and artifacts

Texture, pattern and finish, such as:

Handcrafted wood graining, multi-screened handprints, patterned carpets and fabrics stone, metal, stucco and glass.

Proportion, placement and scale. Maintaining nature's proportions and using neutrals as background support.

Appropriate use of lighting both natural and artificial.

Use the element of surprise!

Ikat fabric courtesy Kravet Inc.

THE END OF THE JOURNEY AND BEGINNING OF THE ADVENTURE
THE STORIES OF THE MODELS

16 three-dimensional computer models
CAPTURING THE ESSENCE OF NATURE'S *LUMINOSITY*
HARNESSING THE POWER OF CONTRAST

These are mini narratives within an overall story of color. Each model is a stage set, a tale with it's own beginning, middle and end. Some are nostalgic, representing a moment in time, memory and place. Others express a range of emotions or connection with family and friends. Each model is designed to honor colors and light specific to that geographic area. My hope is that telling these stories, you the reader will be encouraged to use this new color approach to tell your own stories — your own life, work or environment.

The **JCCS Power Palette** colors for each model were chosen by connecting with the essence of each natural environment, landscape or cityscape. The **JCCS Undertone Color Wheels** are various combinations of **JCCS Composite Color Wheels**, applying the four contrast elements (values, colors, movement and lighting) to capture the sense of *luminosity* or animation present in nature.

Some of the models mirror color proportions of the scene, while others reverse the order of support and focus. I often began with one approach and changed direction in the middle, allowing each model to tell me what it wanted to be (thank you, Louis Kahn).

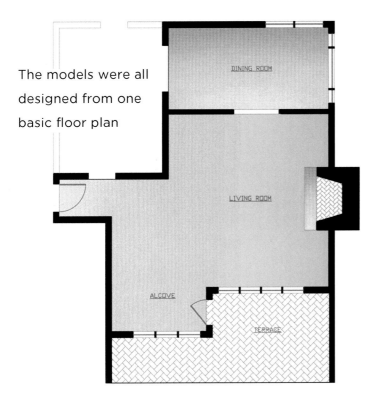

The models were all designed from one basic floor plan

Hues from the eight **JCCS Color Wheels** are illustrated as squares on each photograph, forming a simplified guide to reflect the colors as I perceive them in that scene.

The **JCCS Power Palette** reflects the proportion of each color used in the model.

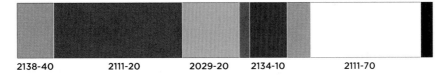

2138-40   2111-20   2029-20   2134-10   2111-70

The combined **JCCS Undertone Color Wheels** for each model were assembled after models were complete. Though unplanned, most of the models resolved using opposite *masstones* and/or *undertones* of all four colors (yellow, red, blue and green).

16 HIGH/LOW CONTRAST MODELS

BASED ON *JCCS POWER PALETTES*

PART FOUR

PART FOUR - 16 HIGH CONTRAST/LOW CONTRAST MODELS

Nature as inspiration for interior design:

Consider an interior as a work of art that combines light and personal memory with the essence of a landscape or cityscape's environment.

YOU BRAVED THE JOURNEY

NOW JOIN ME IN AN ADVENTURE OF DREAMS, NOSTALGIA, DISCOVERY, CONNECTIONS AND SURPRISE.

THE MANY FACES OF
GREEN

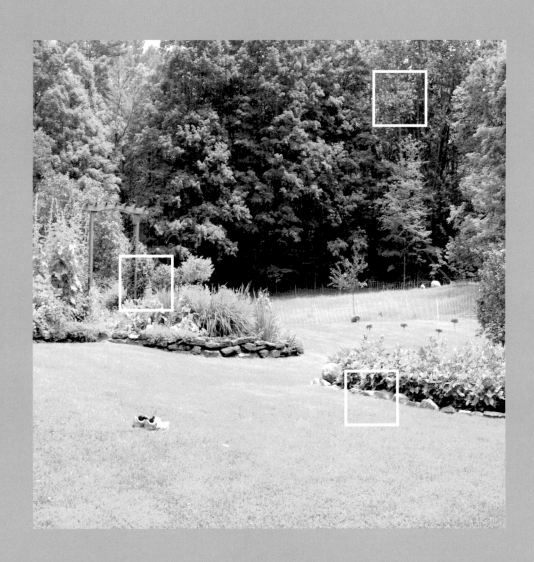

CASE STUDY 2.2
HIGH CONTRAST ELEGANCE IN THE CONNECTICUT WOODS

THE INSPIRATION:

Life in a living painting, where intense colors and trees convey a sense of shelter.

When I return, I am home.

I feel complete.

Value Contrast: HIGH
Lighting Contrast: HIGH

G/Y/W

2029-20

R/B/W

2111-70

G/Y/C

2138-40

B/R/W

2137-20

LIVING ROOM:

All seasons are celebrated in this interior. The vivid contrasts of value, color, texture and lighting highlight the lush green leave of summer and the inevitable white of winter (sofas and wood paneled dado). An elegant panoramic mural, Décor Chinois (courtesy Zuber, France) is a tribute to Spring. See facing page for mural information.

Warm earth tones for the main background areas (walls and flooring) honor nature's proportions, supporting (structurally and esthetically) the green elements. White sofas and paneling provide maximum luminance to balance sparse light filtered through the leaves.

JCCS POWER PALETTE: LIVING ROOM

2138-40   2111-20   2029-20   2134-10   2111-70

Papier peint panoramique « Décor Chinois » crée par la manufacture ZUBER (France) en 1932. Ce décor est toujours, actuellement, imprimé avec les techniques et le matériel ancien d'origine (387 planches de bois sculptées, classées monuments historiques). Copyright (reproduction interdite).

Wallpaper panoramic, Décor Chinois manufactured by Zuber (France) 1932. This mural is still currently printed using the old original equipment and techniques. (387 carved wood blocks classified as historical monuments). Copyright (reproduction forbidden).

DINING ROOM:

The movement of texture and pattern captures the highlights and shadows of sunlight through the trees.

Materials include polished cotton drapery, wood parquet flooring, open floral patterns and a textured rug.

JCCS POWER PALETTE: DINING ROOM

| 2138-40 | 2111-20 | 2029-20 | 2134-10 | 2111-70 |

JCCS UNDERTONE COLOR WHEEL:

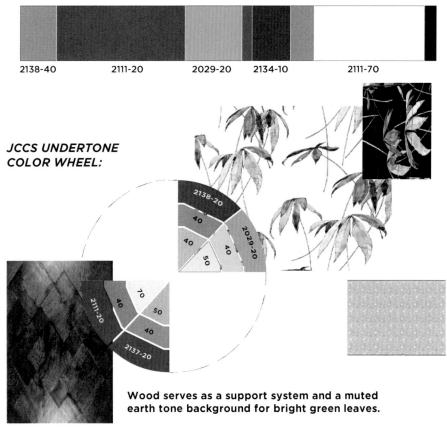

Wood serves as a support system and a muted earth tone background for bright green leaves.

CASE STUDY 1.6 WESTCHESTER, NY
LOW CONTRAST

THE INSPIRATION:

Simplicity and peace in a pine forest.

JCCS UNDERTONE
COLOR WHEEL:

JCCS POWER PALETTE:

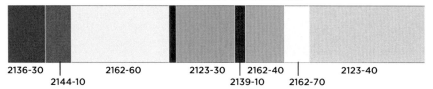

2136-30 | 2162-60 | 2123-30 | 2162-40 | 2123-40

2144-10 | 2139-10 | 2162-70

THE LIVING SPACE:

This space is warmly minimal. The luxury of contemporary furnishings mixes with the architecture of glass and steel artfully in tune with serene surroundings.

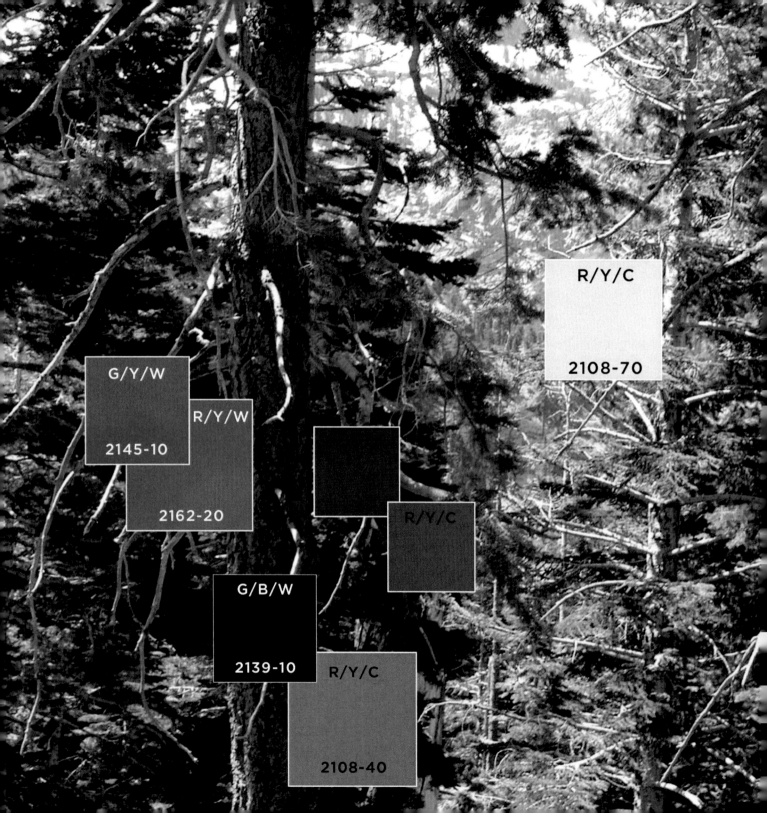

CASE STUDY 1.7 PINE FOREST
LOW CONTRAST

THE INSPIRATION: NOSTALGIA

Reviving the glory of innovative 1940's and 50's mid-century modern design, this palette of wood, stone and steel is a perfect backdrop for furnishings as timeless as a pine forest. Shadows from sunlight filtering through trees create their own unique palette. Songbirds and squirrels are integral to this scene.

JCCS POWER PALETTE:

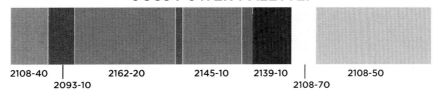

2108-40   2162-20   2145-10   2139-10   2108-50

2093-10   2108-70

JCCS UNDERTONE COLOR WHEEL :

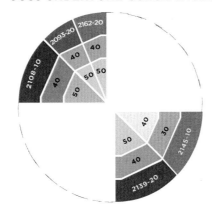

CASE STUDY 2.8 VERMONT MEADOW
HIGH CONTRAST

THE INSPIRATION:

These are memories of a family trip to a Vermont farmhouse.

The mesmerizing jewel colors of summer were inspired by an Arcadian setting of rolling hills, wild grasses and colorful flowers bordered with a background of evergreens.

JCCS UNDERTONE COLOR WHEEL :

JCCS POWER PALETTE:

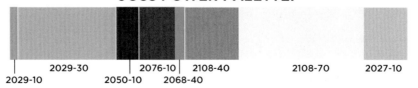

2029-10   2029-30   2050-10   2076-10   2108-40   2068-40   2108-70   2027-10

THE MANY FACES OF
BLUE

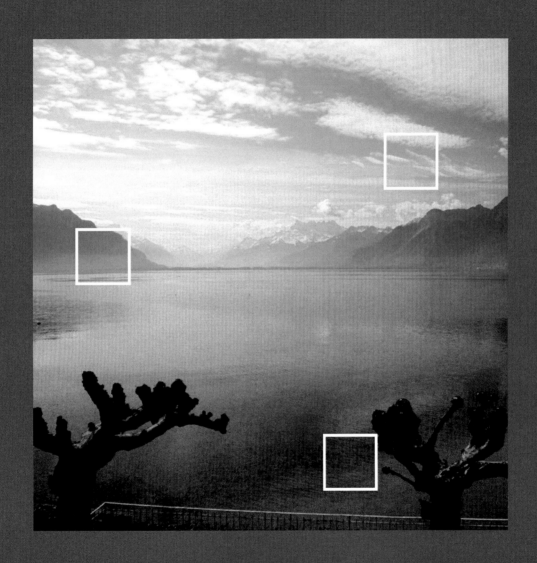

CASE STUDY 4.1 BIG SUR, CA
HIGH CONTRAST

THE INSPIRATION:

I tried to capture the beauty, power and movement of sunlit ocean waves to the home by transforming a deck into a stylish alfresco dining experience. Deep blue/greens are the dominant colors, enriched by combinations of the warm/cool neutrals of the sand and rocks. Minimal red accents complete the palette.

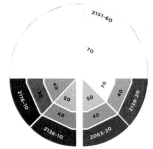

JCCS UNDERTONE COLOR WHEEL :

JCCS POWER PALETTE:

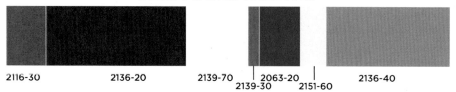

2116-30   2136-20   2139-70   2063-20   2136-40
                               2139-30   2151-60

G/B/W

2139-70

B/G/C

2135-40

B/R/C

2136-30

R/B/W

2173-10

CASE STUDY 2.1 LAKE TAHOE, NV
HIGH CONTRAST

THE INSPIRATION:

The blues of a sparkling lake, mountain and sky blend naturally with colorful boats and hand-hewn wood posts and railings. Combined with a trip to the surrounding vineyards, this rustic vacation area revived my natural reverence for custom cabinetry and old world detailing.

JCCS POWER PALETTE:

2106-10   2136-30   2139-70   2173-10   2135-40

JCCS UNDERTONE COLOR WHEEL :

Seven examples of computer-based art from a talented family member animate the walls and bookcase shelving.

CASE STUDY 1.5 LAKE GENEVA, SWITZERLAND
LOW CONTRAST

JCCS POWER PALETTE:

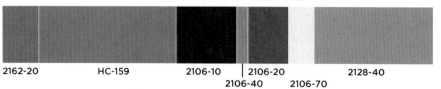

2162-20   HC-159   2106-10   2106-20   2128-40

2106-40   2106-70

B/G/C
2128-40

B/R/W
HC-159

R/B/W
2106-10

R/B/W
2106-40

R/Y/W
2162-20

THE INSPIRATION:

A rare view of Lake Geneva from a dining room.

The many blues of sky, lake and mountains expand and disappear artfully, masking where heaven stops and earth begins.

JCCS UNDERTONE COLOR WHEEL :

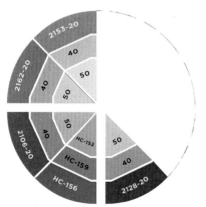

2153-20
40
50
2162-20
40
50
50
40
2106-20
HC-152
50
HC-159
40
HC-156
2128-20

THE MANY FACES OF
RED

CASE STUDY 1.4 VILLAGE DE CULLY, SWITZERLAND
HIGH CONTRAST

THE INSPIRATION: This interior is a tribute to the hospitality of family living near Nestle's hometown of Vevey, Switzerland. I interpreted the scene as an antiquarian fantasy in an Alpine hideaway — a tapestry of rustic elegance and soft, subtle masculinity. The red clay roofs complement the stunning views of the Lake Geneva, where the blues of water and sky perfectly blend.

JCCS POWER PALETTE:

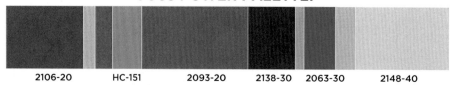

| 2106-20 | HC-151 | 2093-20 | 2138-30 | 2063-30 | 2148-40 |

JCCS UNDERTONE COLOR WHEEL :

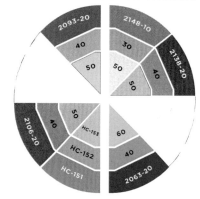

Y/R/C
2093-60

Y/R/C
006-30

G/B/C
2063-30

Y/R/C

2093-30

G/Y/W

2144-10

JCCS POWER PALETTE:

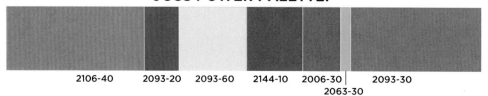

2106-40 2093-20 2093-60 2144-10 2006-30 2093-30

2063-30

Y/R/W

2106-40

CASE STUDY 1.3 SEDONA, AZ
HIGH CONTRAST

THE INSPIRATION:

Sedona is filled with memories of visits with friends exploring Indian caves, the dramatic rhythm of red sandstone architecture, the beat of a jazz ensemble, and the powerful restorative energy of the desert.

JCCS UNDERTONE
COLOR WHEEL :

THE MANY FACES OF
YELLOW

CASE STUDY 2.10 CALIFORNIA WILD FLOWERS
HIGH CONTRAST

THE INSPIRATION:

This image showcases the irresistible hardiness and overwhelming beauty of wildflowers. This is a place that moves me, that delights all the senses, and inspired me to create a yellow/red and green/blue palette reconnecting with the joy of rebirth.

JCCS POWER PALETTE:

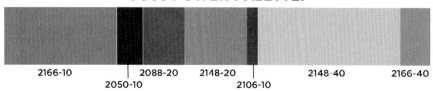

JCCS UNDERTONE COLOR WHEEL :

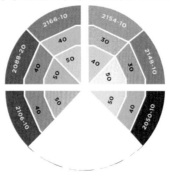

CASE STUDY 2.10 CALIFORNIA WILD FLOWERS
HIGH CONTRAST

CASE STUDY 2.6 SANTA MONICA, CA
LOW CONTRAST

THE INSPIRATION:

The photograph captures fun at the beach and a heavenly vacation condo on the West coast with sweeping ocean views. The palette is a low contrast background of yellow sandy beach tones offset by blue/greens of the ocean and green/yellow shrubs. Grab your surf board and jump in, or breathe in the salt air while resting in a deck chair.

JCCS POWER PALETTE:

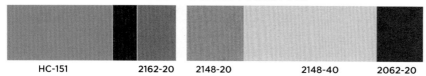

HC-151   2162-20   2148-20   2148-40   2062-20

JCCS UNDERTONE COLOR WHEEL :

2162-20
40
50

2148-20
40
50

HC-153
HC-152
HC - 151

50
40
2062-20

CITISCAPES

LOW CONTRAST/HIGH CONTRAST COMBINATIONS OF YELLOW, RED, BLUE AND GREEN

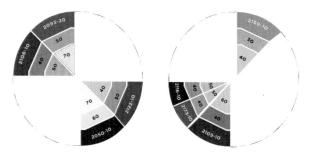

CASE STUDY 1.0 TOKYO, JAPAN
HIGH CONTRAST

THE INSPIRATION:

The design of this interior space, like jazz, is improvising on a theme. The model illustrates my experience connecting color/texture contrast with modern jazz chords and harmony.

R/B/W
2109-40

R/B/W
2173-10

R/B/C
2116-10

Y/R/W
2106-10

Y/R/W
2159-30

JCCS POWER PALETTE:

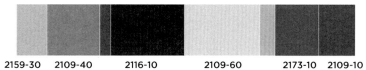

2159-30 2109-40 2116-10 2109-60 2173-10 2109-10

JCCS UNDERTONE COLOR WHEEL :

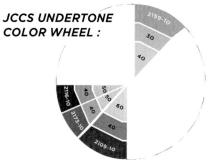

2159-10
30
40
50 50 60
2116-10
40
40
2173-10
40
2109-10

CASE STUDY 2.3 PARIS, FRANCE - 6th Arrondissement
HIGH CONTRAST

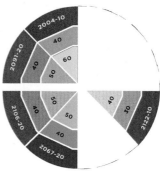

JCCS UNDERTONE
COLOR WHEEL :

THE INSPIRATION:

Paris combines memories of friendship, adventure, exploration of historic St. Sulpice Church and Saint-Germain Abbey, and shared food and wine with friends in the local cafes. The varied colors of this beautiful city are a challenge to capture.

JCCS POWER PALETTE:

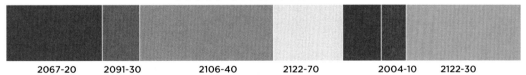

2067-20   2091-30   2106-40   2122-70   2004-10   2122-30

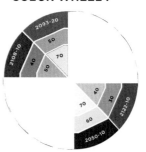

JCCS UNDERTONE COLOR WHEEL :

THE INSPIRATION:

Life is full of surprises. Sharing a trip to the American Institute of Architects convention with family members inspired this flight of fancy, a free-spirited combination of traditional furnishings with a Mies Van der Rohe chaise. A leopard on the balcony completes the picture.

JCCS POWER PALETTE:

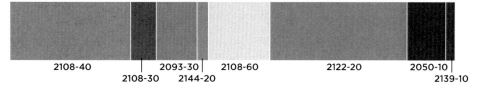

2108-40 2093-30 2108-60 2122-20 2050-10

2108-30 2144-20 2139-10

131

CASE STUDY 3.1 NIGHT LIGHTS IN THE CITY SYDNEY, AU
LOW CONTRAST

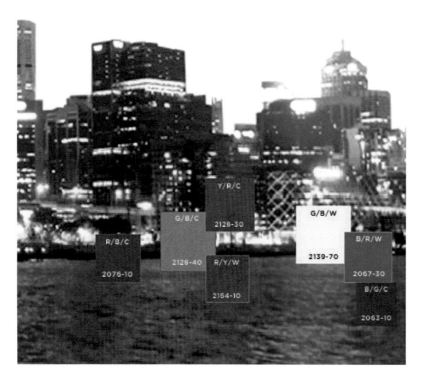

JCCS UNDERTONE COLOR WHEEL :

THE INSPIRATION:

This city at night captured my imagination. Shimmering blue, red and white lights of the buildings reflected in the water, demanding expression and a dramatic masculine palette.

JCCS POWER PALETTE:

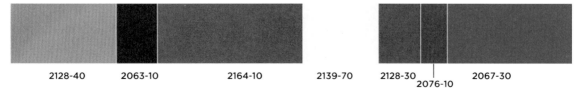

2128-40   2063-10   2164-10   2139-70   2128-30   2067-30
                                                  2076-10

CASE STUDY 2.7 EAST RIVER, WILLIAMSBURG BRIDGE
LOW CONTRAST

THE INSPIRATION:

This is the quieter side of the New York City's boroughs, a view of Williamsburg Bridge from a water taxi drop-off in Brooklyn. This is a sophisticated low-contrast study in earth tones combining cool blues and warm red neutrals.

JCCS POWER PALETTE:

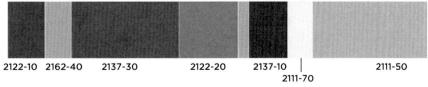

2122-10 2162-40 2137-30   2122-20 2137-10   2111-50
                                                2111-70

JCCS UNDERTONE COLOR WHEEL :

SUMMARY OF THE 16 *JCCS UNDERTONE COLOR WHEELS*
Combinations of *JCCS COMPOSITE COLOR WHEELS*

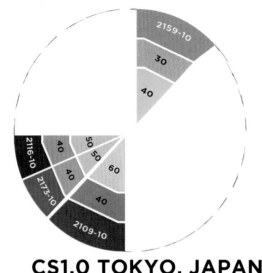

CS1.0 TOKYO, JAPAN

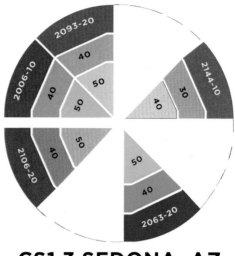

CS1.3 SEDONA, AZ

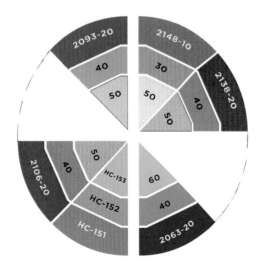

CS1.4 VILLAGE DE CULLY, SWITZERLAND

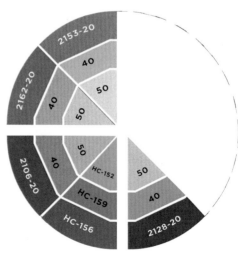

CS1.5 LAKE GENEVA, SWITZERLAND

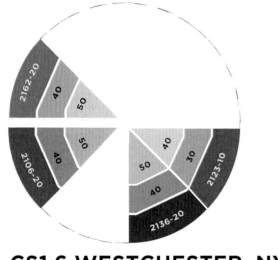

CS1.6 WESTCHESTER, NY

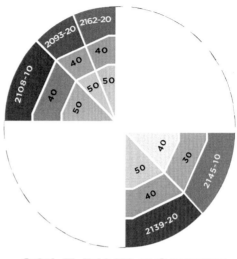

CS1.7 PINE FOREST

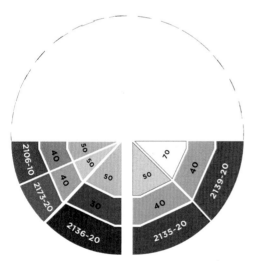

CS2.1 LAKE TAHOE, NV

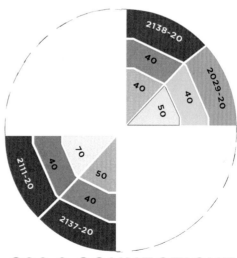

CS2.2 CONNECTICUT

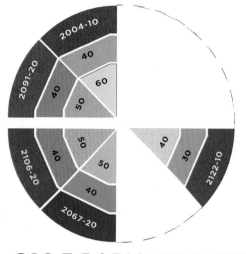

CS2.3 PARIS, FRANCE

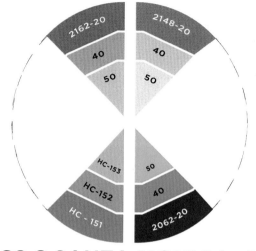

CS2.6 SANTA MONICA, CA

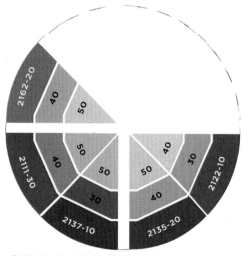

CS2.7 EAST RIVER, NY

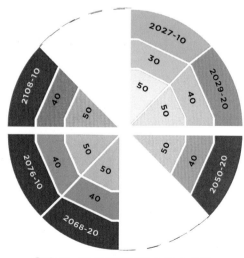

CS2.8 VERMONT

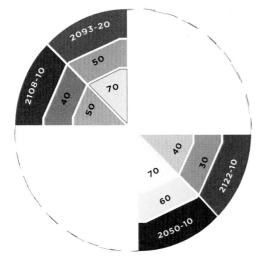

CS2.9 SAN FRANCISCO, CA

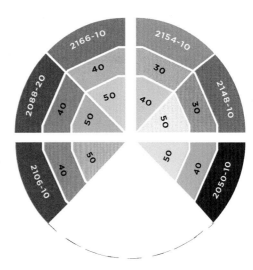

CS2.10 CALIFORNIA WILD FLOWERS

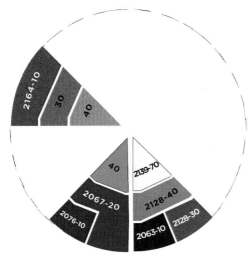

CS3.1 CITY AT NIGHT SYDNEY, AU

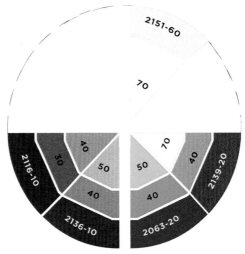

CS4.1 BIG SUR, CA

PAINT COLOR NAME/NUMBER CROSS REFERENCE:

Sun Warm 1A

2004-10 Deep Rose
2004-40 Pink Starburst
2004-50 Baby Girl
2022-10 Yellow
2022-40 Banana Yellow
2022-50 Sundance
2024-10 Chartreuse
2024-30 Citron
2024-50 Jaspar Yellow
2029-20 Baby Fern
2029-40 Stem Green
2029-50 Potpourri Green
2034-20 Vine Green
2034-40 Cedar Green
2034-50 Acadia Green
2049-20 Oasis Blue
2049-40 Peacock Blue
2049-50 Spectra Blue
2067-20 Starry Night Blue
2067-40 Blue Lapis
2067-50 Summer Blue
2077-10 Magenta
2077-40 Spring Azalea
2077-50 Pretty Pink

Mineral Warm 1B

2088-20 Country Lane
2088-40 Persimmon
2088-50 Cool Lava
2147-10 Oregano
2147-30 Jalapeno Pepper
2147-40 Dill Pickle
2159-10 Dash of Curry
2159-30 Apple Crisp
2159-40 Amber Waves
2167-20 Pumpkin Pie
2167-40 Toffee Orange
2167-50 Perfect Peach
2173-20 Tawny Rose
2173-40 Antique Rose
2173-50 Coral Dust
HC-127 Fairmont Green
HC-128 Clearspring Green
HC-129 Southfield Green
HC-152 Whipple Blue
HC-153 Marlboro Blue
HC-156 Van Deusen Blue
AC-22 Nantucket Fog
AC-23 James River Gray
AC-24 Charlotte Slate

Earth Tones Warm 1C

1568 Quarry Rock
1566 Stonybrook
1565 Mount Saint Anne
2106-20 Auberge
2106-40 Cougar Brown
2106-50 Driftscape Tan
2137-20 Char Brown
2137-40 Desert Twilight
2137-50 Sea Haze
2139-20 Dakota Woods Green
2139-40 Heather Gray
2139-50 Silver Marlin
2144-20 Eucalyptus Leaf
2144-30 Rosemary Sprig
2144-50 Silken Pine
2148-10 Foot Hills
2148-30 Military Tan
2148-50 Sandy White
2160-10 Caramel Corn
2160-30 Maple Sugar
2160-40 Roasted Sesame Seed
2162-10 Autumn Bronze
2162-40 Peanut Shell
2162-50 Arizona Tan

Off Whites Warm 1D

2106-60 Soft Sand
2109-60 Portland Gray
2137-60 Gray Owl
2139-60 Green Tint
2144-60 Cloud Nine
2148-70 Mountain Peak White
2158-60 Lion Yellow
2162-60 Mystic Beige

Sun Cool 2A

2006-10 Merlot Red
2006-40 Glamour Pink
2006-50 Pink Punch
2050-20 Dollar Bill Green
2050-40 Florida Keys Blue
2050-50 Waterfall
2063-20 Down Pour Blue
2063-40 Sailor's Sea Blue
2063-50 Blue Marguerite
2068-20 Grape Gum
2068-40 California Lilac
2068-50 Victorian Trim
2076-10 Crushed Velvet
2076-40 Raspberry Mousse
2076-50 Easter Pink
2145-10 Avocado
424 Scenic View
426 Fresh Grass
427 Napa Vineyards
2154-10 Yellow Oxide
2154-30 Buttercup
2154-40 York Harbor Yellow
2166-10 Gold Rush
2166-40 Soft Pumpkin
2166-50 Creamy Orange

Mineral Cool 2B

2091-20 Rustic Brick
2091-40 Red River Clay
2091-50 Rosy Tan
2093-20 Fresh Clay
2093-40 Belladonna Lily
2093-50 Camellia Pink
2113-20 Pine Cone Brown
2113-40 Cinnamon Slate
2113-50 Mauve Desert
2116-10 Night Shade
2116-30 Cabernet
2116-40 Hazy Lilac
2123-20 Caribbean Teal
2123-30 Sea Star
2123-40 Gossamer Blue
2135-20 Stonecutter
2135-40 Province Blue
2135-50 Soft Chinchilla
2149-20 G.I. Green
2149-40 Timothy Straw
2149-50 Mellowed Ivory
2152-10 Medieval Gold
2152-30 Autumn Gold
2152-40 Golden Tan

Earth Tones Cool 2C

2108-10 Ferret Brown
2108-40 Stardust
2108-50 Silver Fox
2115-10 Appalachian Brown
2115-40 Mauve Blush
2115-50 Iced Mauve
2118-20 Toucan Black
2118-40 Sea Life
2118-50 Excalibur Gray
2122-20 Steep Cliff Gray
2122-30 Cloudy Sky
2122-40 Smoke
2128-20 Abyss
2128-40 Oxford Gray
2128-50 November Skies
2150-20 Lichen Green
2150-30 Savannah Green
2150-50 Hampton Green
2151-20 Golden Chalice
2151-40 Sulfur Yellow
2151-50 Bronzed Beige
2153-20 Corduroy
2153-40 Cork
2153-50 Desert Tan

Off Whites Cool 2D

2070-60 Lavendar Mist
2071-60 Lily Lavendar
2105-60 Acapulco Sane
2122-60 Palest Pistachio
2131-60 Silver Gray
2149-60 White Marigold
2151-60 Linen Sand
2153-60 Rich Cream

Note: the above is a partial cross reference. Check with your local paint store or the website, www.benjaminmoore.com for additional names/numbers and to verify accuracy.

GLOSSARY OF TERMS

Color Terms:

Additive Color - Visible wavelengths of perceived colors in light that, when mixed together, produce white light.

Afterimage - Colors remaining in one's vision after exposure to a light source has ceased.

Contrast - The difference in brightness between an object and its background. Low contrast minimizes the difference, while high contrast maximizes the difference.

Cool Colors - Colors in some commercial paints mixed with a blue base.

LRV - Abbreviation for light reflectance value, which is a measurement of the light or dark aspect of a color. Luminance decreases with lower (5-20) LRV of dark colors, and increases with higher (80-90) LRV of lighter colors.

Luminosity - The magnitude of an object's brightness. In interior design it is a combination of light, color and movement in a material. Natural wood patinas, marble graining and natural dye mixing in hand woven Oriental rugs are examples of luminous materials.

Subtractive Color - Color mixed with pigment beginning with white. With each addition of pigment, more light and color is absorbed (or subtracted) deepening toward black as colors are mixed.

Value - The brightness aspect of color (light, medium or dark) as measured by LRV.

Warm Colors - Colors in some commercial paints mixed with a red base.

JCCS Terms:

JCCS - *Jaroff Contrast Color System*

JCCS Composite Color - Nature's four basic *masstones* of yellow, red, blue, and green used in combination with nature's basic *undertones*.

JCCS Composite Color Wheel - A color wheel based on nature's eight basic composite colors; red/yellow, yellow/red, yellow/green, green/yellow, green/blue, blue/green, blue/red, red/blue. Colors opposite each other on the wheel are *afterimages*.

JCCS Contrast Power Palette - Colors selected from a **JCCS Undertone Color Wheel** and arranged according to the proportion of each color used in a design.

Nature's Masstones - The yellow, red, blue or green color immediately apparent on a surface.

Nature's Undertones - The concealed yellow, red, blue or green color that defines a relationship to the underlying *masstone* adjacent to it on the **JCCS Composite Color Wheel.**

JCCS Undertone Color Wheel - A palette of colors selected from a combination of **JCCS Composite Color Wheels** for a design and arranged on a color wheel based on *afterimage* and desired contrast (low or high).

Temperature - The warm or cool aspect of a color. Every *masstone* and/or composite color has a warm or a cool component.

Earth Tones - The lowest chromatic intensity colors or neutral beiges grays, ivories and taupes.

Mineral Colors - Colors toned down to medium chromatic intensity, less saturated than sun colors.

Off Whites - The lightest values of earth tones or neutral colors.

Sun Colors - The highest intensity and most vivid (saturated) colors. In areas of the Northern Hemisphere lacking in bright sunlight, sun colors are used most effectively as accents or in small proportions.

GLOSSARY OF TERMS (CONT.)

Light Terms:

Ambient Light- General illumination from surrounding light (interior or exterior). Ambient light affects the largest surfaces and conveys a mood of either high or low contrast.

Color Temperature (CCT) – Description of a light source's appearance. Cool lamps have a temperature range from 5,000 to 7,000 degrees Kelvin (K) and are bluish in appearance. Warm lamps have a temperature range from 2,700 to 3,000K and are yellow or red in appearance. The temperature of sunlight at noon is standardized for convenience at 5,600 K for correlation to lamp metrics, but actual noon sunlight will vary depending on geographic location and weather.

CRI - Abbreviation for color rendering index. CRI represents the ability of a light source to render colors across the entire light spectrum. While a high CRI value of 85+ indicates a desirable color rendition range it may render across a broad range of colors well but will not necessarily render a specific color satisfactorily across all temperature (K) ranges.

Daylight - A combination of direct and indirect or diffuse exterior light. A term also used to describe the color rendition of a lamp that is close to the standard white light of high noon.

Direct Light - Hard, sharp light producing highlights and shadows as well as reflected light on surfaces, increasing contrast. Light produced from a point source (the sun or an artificial light fixture).

Focal Light - Light emphasizing objects and surfaces. Focal light creates visual direction and focus, commands attention and holds interest.

Glare - Unshielded or misdirected light, which can be discomforting. Glare can also result from inter-reflection, which reduces contrasts between a surface and light source.

Grazing Lights - Light that bounces illumination off a smooth surface, such as mirror or calm water.

Indirect (Reflected) Light - Light reflecting off surfaces and objects, revealing color, shape and other details. Most of the light we see is reflected light.

Lamp - Technical term for a light bulb.

LED Lighting - Illumination from light emitting diode lamps.

Luminance - Perceived brightness or intensity of light reflected from or transmitted through all surfaces in a space.

Metamerism - The variation or mismatching of colored objects and materials under different light sources.

Reflectance - The degree of light leaving a surface, or the ability of a surface to re-transmit light independent of the light itself reaching the surface.

Diffuse Reflection - Dispersed, multidirectional light reflected equally at all angles. Diffuse reflections between surfaces and objects filling in shadows, reducing contrast and creating a uniform luminance similar to the sky when conditions are overcast.

Specular Reflection - Light bouncing off a smooth surface at the same angle at which light strikes the surface, generally from a mirror or polished material.

Semi-specular Reflection - Light reflected from matte surfaces and uniformly bright from all angles. Though some light is reflected diffusely and some specularly, most light is semi-specular.

Sparkle Light - Directional light that produces highlights and creates focus or commands attention to an object or surface.

Transmission - The ability of a material or object to allow light to pass through independent of the amount of light reaching the surface or object.

PHOTO CREDITS:

George Abraham

Chobe Lodge, Uganda/107 Case study 1.4

Richard Buday FAIA

Lake Geneva/26, 51, 93, 102, 103

Tom Buday

Clouds/38

Utah/45, 57

Sandra Castleman

Hawaiian Rainbow/40

Dreamstime.com

© Pepeemilio

Jazz Photo/124 Case study 1.0

Joan Facer

Lake Garda, Italy/104

Reagan James

Photography © Mishone Feigin

Vision/40

Michael Kurcfeld

Paris/123, 126

Sam Lubell

Red Sunset/31, 44, 56

Herman Miller Inc/ *www.hermanmiller.com*

Eames Lounge Chair & Ottoman,

Eames Molded Plywood Chair, Eames Walnut Stool/39

Michael Buday

Olympos, Turkey/32

Harvey Newman

Pine Forest/28, 51, 52, 53, 57, 68/69, 71, 72, 80, 84

Half Dome Yosemite/4, 9, 24, 25, 27, 45, 52, 53, 56, 65

Wildflowers/32, 33, 44, 112, 113, 114

Santa Monica/52, 53, 57, 112

Sunset/57

Podium Browser

Tokyo Panorama/122, 125

Sydney,AU/92, 134

Shutterstock.com

Big Sur/26, 35, 36, 38, 56, 92, 94

Sedona/4, 30, 104, 108

Cassandra Tondro

Raindrops/38

Ventura Beach/32, 37, 40, 112, 118

Zuber, France

Wallpaper Panoramic, Décor Chinois/77

Manufactured by Zuber (France) 1932.

ART CREDITS:

All Artwork in the models © by permission of the following artists:

Bob Boreman/
bobboremanart.com
Green Abstract/81, 83 Case study 1.6
Mural/82 Case study 1.6
Tulips/86 Case study 1.7
Blue Landscape/103 Case study 1.5
Sun Flowers/115 Case study 2.10
Floral Monoprint/116 Case study 2.10
Abstract Red, White, Blue
/65, 128 Case study 2.3

Gene Buday/ *genebuday.com*
Dancers 1, 2, 3, 4, 5, 100/101 Case study 2.1
Portrait 1/99, 100 Case study 2.1
Portrait 2/99 Case study 2.1

Edison T. Crayne/ *Craynearts.com*
Willow Pond/132 Case study 2.9
McClaren Pond/34, 136 Case study 3.1
Paint the Lake/138, 140 Case study 2.7
Waiting for the Sun/136 Case study 3.1

Victoria Crayne/ *Craynearts.com*
Quilt, "With Apologies to Van Gogh"
/110 Case study 1.3

Doug Edge/ *dougedgestudio.com*
DE3/109 Case study 1.3
DE4/34

Joshua Elias/ *joshuaelias.com*
The Earth, The Spirit/131 Case study 2.9
Photography © Matthew Ullman,
go4pdi@sbcglobal.net

Sylvia Greer/
sylvia@artwworks.com
Chinese/115 Case study 2.10

Arleen Hendler/
arleenhendler@yahoo.com
The Culver/110 Case study 1.3
Reel Joy/139 Case study 2.7

Reagan James/
reagan.jar@gmail.com
Woman in Water/97 Case study 4.1
/127 Case study 2.3

Cinthia Joyce/ *cinthiajoyce.com*
Aqua 8062/119 Case study 2.6
Woman at a Bar/133 Case study 2.9
Rooster/131, 133 Case study 2.9
View from the Pier/121 Case study 2.6

Tom Lieber/ *tomlieberartist.com*
Pastel/107 Case study 1.4,
Thumbs 1844/107 Case study 1.4
/95 Case study 4.1
Turquoise/107 Case study 1.4
Ellipse 4/81, 83 Case study 1.6
/120 Case study 2.6
/141 Case study 2.7
Red Wide/133 Case study 2.9

Margaret Noesner/
manoesner@verizon.net
Horse/115 Case study 2.10

Carole Spence/ *carolespence.com*
Mail Call 8/89 Case study 2.8

Cassandra Tondro/ *Tondro.com*
A Rose by Any Other Name
/89 Case study 2.8
Red, Olive Abstract/90 Case study 2.8
Into Light 2/129 Case study 2.3
Demo/115 Case study 2.10

G/Y/W
2029-20

R/B/W
2111-70

G/Y/C
2138-40

B/R/W
2137-20